Tracing the Path of a Sunken Slave Ship,
a Bitter Past, and a Rich Legacy

SHACKLES
FROM THE
DEEP

PULITZER
PRIZE–WINNING
AUTHOR
MICHAEL H.
COTTMAN

NATIONAL
GEOGRAPHIC

For librarians and teachers:
ngchildrensbooks.org

More for kids from
National Geographic:
kids.nationalgeographic.com

For information about special
discounts for bulk purchases,
please contact National
Geographic Books Special Sales:
specialsales@natgeo.com

For rights or permissions inqui-
ries, please contact National
Geographic Books Subsidiary
Rights: bookrights@natgeo.com

Designed by James Hiscott, Jr.
Text set in Minion Pro
Display text set in Retro Bold
Standard; Veneer

Hardcover ISBN:
978-1-4263-2663-9
Reinforced library binding
ISBN: 978-1-4263-2664-6

Printed in the United States
of America
16/WOR/1

DEDICATION

For my daughter, Ariane

We have hurdled waves together in the Pacific Ocean, snorkeled in the Gulf of Mexico, smiled at parrotfish in the Caribbean Sea, and talked about life along the Chesapeake Bay. What wonderful father-daughter memories. Embrace your sense of adventure and continue to explore the world's magnificent waterways, where you will always find peace. You are a blessing. Love, Dad.

A NOTE ABOUT LANGUAGE

Readers will travel through history with this book and encounter examples of language old and new, respectful and hateful. Between the pages of this book, we present the term "Negro" in quotations from historical source material. Racial epithets of that era remain no less offensive today, but they are a part of the historical record and are used in quotations from the period without censorship.

CONTENTS

FOREWORD

by Geoffrey Canada ~ president of the Harlem Children's Zone

THESE DAYS, when people talk about slavery in the United States, they think of it as ancient history, but for me it's not so distant. That's because I have spoken face-to-face with a slave, my great-grandmother.

She was born just a couple of years before the Emancipation Proclamation, so while she grew up free, she was born into slavery. I only learned about it years after her death, and I was stunned. Suddenly slavery was very real to me. Then something else happened and made me realize slavery is a legacy that's part of who I am today.

For a segment on the PBS television show *Finding Your Roots,* historian and Harvard University professor Henry Louis Gates, Jr., and his staff did a thorough search of my genetic makeup and my family history. My father had left our family when I was very young, so I had a lot of unanswered questions about my last name and genealogy. Like the characters in the comic books I loved as a young boy, I also wanted to know my "origin story," to learn what I was made of, what slice of the African-American experience I read about in school was my own. What Gates uncovered was astounding to me.

The researchers dug into old records to see where my father's surname and family had come from. After some twists and turns, they were finally able to trace the family back to the slave operations of a rural plantation in Virginia run by the Cannady family.

I traveled with Gates to the area where my ancestors were held as slaves. It was disturbing to think of my own flesh and blood living there, people like my great-grandmother, unable to read or write or even know where they were in this strange foreign place. As I walked through the land, surrounded by hills and hearing dogs barking in the distance, I felt in my gut how trapped and frightened my ancestors might have felt there. Even though I now know where my ancestors lived during slavery, I still have so many questions: How long were they there? How were they treated? Did they sail across the Atlantic on a ship like the *Henrietta Marie*? Sadly that ancestry is untraceable for so many African Americans, who lost their history along with their freedom and dignity.

For me, discovering my own family story highlighted the closeness of history—and that our collective history helps shape us into who we are today.

The Emancipation Proclamation ended the practice of slavery more than 150 years ago, but the tragic legacy of those prior decades continues to cast a long shadow over our present.

Like author Michael Cottman, and the intrepid treasure hunters and marine archaeologists unearthing the wreck of the *Henrietta Marie* under the sea, it's critical for *all* of us to investigate the past—to learn what ground we stand on as we step forward into the future.

Timeline of the
Henrietta Marie

1698 ~ The first voyage of the *Henrietta Marie*.
The ship arrives in Barbados carrying
250 enslaved African people.

1699 ~ The *Henrietta Marie* sails from London on
its second voyage.

1700 ~ The *Henrietta Marie* arrives in Jamaica
with 190 enslaved African people.

1700 ~ The *Henrietta Marie* sinks in a storm on
New Ground Reef, near Key West, Florida.

1972 ~ Underwater treasure hunter Moe Molinar
finds shackles and a cannon from the
"English Wreck" on New Ground Reef.

1983 ~ David Moore discovers the watch bell from
the *Henrietta Marie*.

1991 ~ Corey Malcom leads an excavation of
the *Henrietta Marie*, finding more shackles,
pewter basins, cannonballs, elephant tusks,
glass bottles, a musket, and an iron cannon.

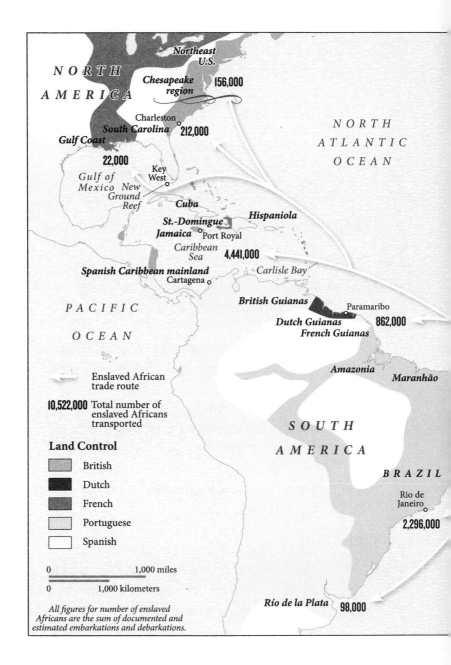

12

NORTH AMERICA

Northeast U.S.

Chesapeake region **156,000**

Charleston ○
South Carolina **212,000**
Gulf Coast
22,000

NORTH ATLANTIC OCEAN

Gulf of Mexico New Ground Reef

Key West ○

Cuba

Hispaniola

St.-Domingue ○
Jamaica ○ Port Royal

Caribbean Sea **4,441,000**

Carlisle Bay

Spanish Caribbean mainland
Cartagena ○

British Guianas

Paramaribo ○

PACIFIC OCEAN

Dutch Guianas
French Guianas **862,000**

Amazonia

Maranhão

SOUTH AMERICA

BRAZIL

→ Enslaved African trade route

10,522,000 Total number of enslaved Africans transported

Land Control

British
Dutch
French
Portuguese
Spanish

Rio de Janeiro ○

2,296,000

0   1,000 miles
0   1,000 kilometers

All figures for number of enslaved Africans are the sum of documented and estimated embarkations and debarkations.

Río de la Plata **98,000**

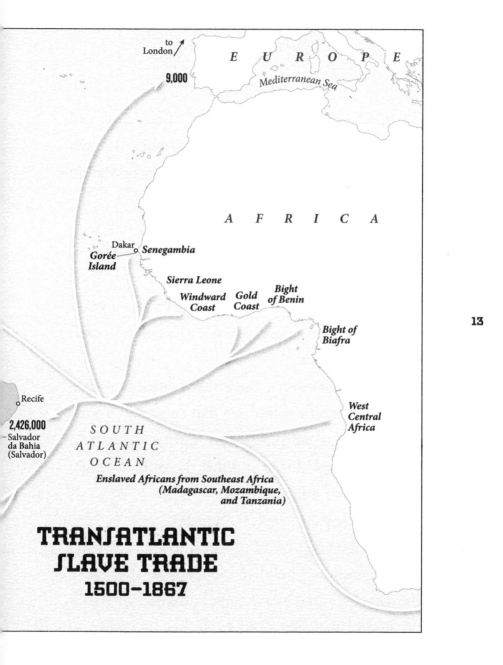

to London
9,000

EUROPE
Mediterranean Sea

AFRICA

Dakar
Gorée Island — Senegambia
Sierra Leone
Windward Coast Gold Coast Bight of Benin
Bight of Biafra

Recife
2,426,000
Salvador da Bahia (Salvador)

West Central Africa

SOUTH ATLANTIC OCEAN

Enslaved Africans from Southeast Africa
(Madagascar, Mozambique, and Tanzania)

TRANSATLANTIC SLAVE TRADE
1500–1867

PROLOGUE

"WHERE IS YOUR VILLAGE?" the young girl asked me. It was 1997 and I was traveling through Timbuktu, which is a city in the country of Mali in West Africa.

While there, I met this girl, 10 years old, with brown skin and tiny earrings. She lived on the banks of the Niger River.

She was curious about me. She probably noticed my unusual clothes and correctly concluded that I wasn't from there.

"I'm from Detroit, in the United States," I told her.

She paused, then told me that she came from a family of kings and queens, that the men in her tribe were the village elders, and that the women taught young girls to read and write.

"Who are your people?" she asked.

This time I paused. I didn't really have an answer to her question. I told her about a slave ship called the *Henrietta Marie* and how I was led to Africa because of this ship. And I told her that we're all

connected through the spirits of our African ancestors regardless of where we live or which villages or
towns we come from.

She smiled and whispered to her friends in her
West African dialect. I didn't understand what she
was saying, but all of the children smiled and waved
to me as I left their village.

Are my people Igbo from Nigeria, or Fulani from
Mali, or Wolof from Senegal, or Ashanti from Ghana?
Sadly, I may never know. But somehow, as I stood
on African soil, I felt at home.

CHAPTER 1

Instruction in youth is like engraving in stone. ~ Moroccan proverb

I ZIP UP MY WET SUIT,

adjust my mask, strap on my steel scuba tanks, breathe into my regulator, and slowly descend into a vast underwater world of translucent jellyfish, wide-winged manta rays, and giant sea turtles.

The gentle underwater currents nudge me along the colorful reefs—past the deep purple sea fans, the bursting orange coral heads, and the white tubular anemones that sway in the sea silt.

Bright yellow angelfish swim a few feet above me in synchronized rhythm.

Nearby, a shiny barracuda crosses my path with a snapped fishing line dangling from his mouth. He had no doubt stripped the bait from an unsuspecting fisherman and fled quickly into the deep.

In the distance, I watch the ocean's most feared predators zig-zagging in and out of the shadows—the saw-toothed blacktip sharks that are more interested in observing the bubble-breathing scuba divers than confronting them.

I exhale and drop slowly to the sandy ocean floor.

I am a deep-sea scuba diver.

My love of the sea started when I was young. I grew up in a mostly black, middle-class neighborhood in Detroit, Michigan. In the evenings, I would sit in the living room watching *Sea Hunt*, an underwater adventure television program that aired when I was a boy in the late 1950s and early '60s.

I enjoyed *Sea Hunt* because it was unlike anything I had ever seen. It featured ocean exploration and sunken ships and treasure—and I decided right then that I too would one day explore shipwrecks in distant oceans.

There was just one problem. Little boys from Detroit didn't know much about scuba diving.

I was the only kid in my neighborhood who talked about diving, and I never missed an episode of this television show. My friends played basketball, football, and baseball. I enjoyed playing sports, too, but I yearned for travel and adventure.

For me, *Sea Hunt* was an escape of sorts, something to help me cope with the atmosphere surrounding the violent civil rights marches and demonstrations that were happening in Detroit at the time.

I didn't know how to swim, but luckily my mother was not only supportive, she was also an excellent swimmer. She took me to the local pool and, in the protective shallow end, she taught me the "front crawl" and the breaststroke. Eventually she felt I was ready to master the deep end of the pool. I wasn't so sure.

As I stood tentatively at the edge of the pool, looking into 10 terrifying feet of water, without warning, she pushed me in! I wish I could say that I swam around the pool with the grace of a delicate swan, but no—I sputtered and flailed to the side of the pool and clutched the cold tile as if it were a lifeline, gaping up at my mom and her sly smile.

But then, once my heart stopped racing, I looked back at the water and took a deep breath. I slipped under the surface and swam the entire length of the pool for the very first time. My mom told me how proud she was, and we drove home laughing about my first experience in the deep.

I've been swimming ever since.

This is a story about how my love of swimming, and later deep-sea diving, led me on a journey to three continents as I helped uncover the mystery surrounding a little-known 17th-century shipwreck. It's about how I, along with others, pieced together a 300-year-old transatlantic puzzle that would teach me about myself—and where I came from. But more than that, it's the untold story of millions of African people taken as captives to the New World, whose names and faces have been erased and eradicated by time, distance, and history.

CHAPTER 2

A patient person never misses a thing. ~ Moroccan proverb

THE RUSTED STEEL ANCHOR CHAIN

rumbled over the side of the *Virgalona* as the weathered boat engine sputtered to a stop.

Captain Demostenes "Moe" Molinar, a diesel mechanic turned boat captain from Panama and a legend among underwater treasure hunters, was at the helm of the *Virgalona*, his 51-foot salvage boat. He was monitoring the swift currents on the surface before making his decision to dive into the murky Gulf of Mexico.

It was July 1972 and Moe was searching for underwater treasure—and lots of it. He was looking for the *Nuestra Señora de Atocha*, a three-masted Spanish galleon that sank in 1622 after slamming into coral reefs during a hurricane. At the time, the ship was carrying chests full of gold, silver, and precious stones from Central and South America back to Spain. Moe and his team knew that there was so much treasure aboard that it took workers back then two months to record all the jewels and load it. Moe was hired by famed treasure hunter Mel Fisher to find glitter in the sand.

Over the course of more than a decade, Moe and his crew had researched the suspected location of the *Nuestra Señora de Atocha* by using a whole slew of technology and instruments, including side-scan sonars, metal detectors, and cesium magnetometers to search for piles of iron from Spanish galleons.

Moe and his mates were pretty confident that the fractured Spanish galleon rested on the ocean floor near an area known as the Marquesas Keys, about 25 miles west of Key West, Florida.

After Christopher Columbus's first voyage to the New World in 1492, the Spanish set out to conquer foreign colonies, and they would amass an array of riches during their voyages. During these roughly 400 years of plundering the New World, hurricanes occasionally tossed and sank Spain's treasure ships, like the *Nuestra Señora de Atocha,* burying the bounty under layers of sand.

Based on extensive research by Mel Fisher and his family, Moe knew the *Nuestra Señora de Atocha* was within his reach, but locating the exact location of the ship on the seafloor would be like finding a needle in a haystack.

"It's a big ocean out there and the bottom changes regularly," Moe often told his crew.

Despite the odds, Moe was determined to find a cargo of riches.

Moe slipped on his fins, strapped on his scuba mask, popped his regulator into his mouth, and rolled backward off the *Virgalona,* plunging 30 feet into the Gulf of Mexico.

It was a familiar place.

Moe was known worldwide as one of the most accomplished treasure hunters in America—and certainly the most well-known black underwater treasure hunter in modern times.

Moe's buddies say he used mystical abilities to locate underwater treasure when others had simply given up on their searches.

The Gulf of Mexico's surface was choppy, so Moe knew he would need to descend quickly. His crew followed Moe into the water, one by one, and they all dropped under the foamy waves and down to the seafloor.

Swimming among the tall seagrass, Moe was annoyed by a fat-faced grouper that tugged on his regulator hose. The grouper probably confused Moe's coiled scuba hose with the four-foot-long black worms that groupers like to eat. Moe gently pushed the grouper away and used his fins to kick through the silt.

He swam past sea fans, schools of colorful fish, and even sharks that circled nearby. Moe was accustomed to seeing sharks—big sharks, small sharks, aggressive sharks, and the kind of sharks that prefer to be left alone. And some sharks that just won't go away.

On this particular day, Moe was harassed so much by a shark that he almost called off the search, worried for himself and his team.

After the shark finally left, Moe decided to make one last sweep of the shipwreck before calling it a day.

Moe saw something lying on the sand in the shadowy distance. After a few minutes of kicking hard against the current, he reached the object. Moe used his rugged hands to lightly part layers of sand and sediment from what appeared to be ancient relics.

As a veteran underwater treasure hunter, Moe had seen a lot of crazy things in his day, so he wasn't easily surprised. But on that day, Moe was astounded by what he saw.

Moe stared at the small pile of iron caked in rust and limestone. He reached out to touch it. It was hard and menacing, and it sent a chill up his spine.

He gently picked up a large chunk of the iron and, with a sickening feeling, realized what he was holding in his seawater-wrinkled hands: a pair of hardened, ancient shackles—heavy manacles that he knew were designed specifically to handcuff the wrists of enslaved Africans, wrists that—he couldn't help thinking—had probably looked much like his own.

Moe's mind was racing with questions. Why were these shackles on this site? How did they get there?

How long had they been there? He thought it unlikely that they would be from the *Nuestra Señora de Atocha*, which made him wonder, Where did these come from?

The discovery of the shackles made this shipwreck site different from all the other shipwrecks Moe had explored. He plunged his hands into the sand and began unearthing more shackles, several pairs at a time.

Each pair of shackles weighed six pounds and had two holes the size of quarters to hold a 13-inch-long bolt that locked into place to bind someone's wrists tightly and efficiently. They were unyielding and they were sure to cause extreme discomfort and pain.

To give you an idea of how amazing it was that Moe even discovered this tiny mound of lost relics, you have to imagine how it must have been. A whole ocean stretches beneath you as, weightless, you peer hard through murky water and swirling sand, searching for a pinpoint of something slightly out of place—all against a backdrop of an ever shifting seafloor.

As he reached down into the sand again, Moe tugged at another pair of shackles from the pile, but these shackles were different from the others: They were tiny, thin, and almost flimsy, and they fit in the palm of

Moe's hand. He knew that these particular cuffs were designed specifically for the small wrists of children.

Suddenly Moe felt overwhelmed. Who would make handcuffs for children? And what kind of person would use these grisly tools? Where did these shackles come from and how many people had worn them?

Not all treasure is about glitter. Sometimes, along the route to discovery, we find something that is more valuable than precious stones. Sometimes we learn something about our human story and ourselves.

Moe's discovery in and of itself was extraordinary—but it was even more so because of this: 300 years after those shackles were used to bind African people aboard a sweltering slave ship, the first man to touch those same shackles was Moe, a free black man.

While Moe and the crew began to survey the site in the Marquesas known as the New Ground Reef, they unearthed another artifact: an iron cannon weighing about 800 pounds. Moe was pretty sure he had stumbled upon the remains of a sunken slave ship. He surfaced with the shackles and went to work trying to make sense of what he'd found.

WHO WOULD MAKE HANDCUFFS FOR CHILDREN? AND WHAT KIND OF PERSON WOULD USE THESE GRISLY TOOLS?

It didn't take long before divers, treasure salvagers, and marine archaeologists were all talking about this mysterious shipwreck without a name. It wasn't the *Nuestra Señora,* which Moe would go on to find in 1985. Moe had come across what came to be known only as the "English Wreck."

The artifacts from the English Wreck were unloaded from the *Virgalona* and stored in a laboratory in Key West, Florida. Ten years passed, and it seemed the relics with such mystery and importance might be forgotten and lost to time once again.

CHAPTER 3

The future emerges from the past. ~ Senegalese proverb

WHAT IS KNOWN AS THE

transatlantic slave trade began in 1441, according to historians, when two Portuguese ships sailed the coast of West Africa. They were looking for gold and other goods in Africa. But they discovered that slavery, the buying and selling of people, could be profitable as well. They knew there was a demand for workers to harvest plantations in the Caribbean and to serve as laborers in Europe and South America.

What began as trading for a few African people ultimately evolved into the centuries-long global kidnapping and exploitation of the West African civilization by European nations, including Portugal, Spain, England, France, and the Netherlands. By the start of the 16th century, according to some historians, tens of thousands of African people had been transported to Europe and islands in the Atlantic Ocean. They were chained inside jam-packed slave ships and would never see Africa—their homeland—again.

The seed of fear was sowed into the fabric of the once vibrant West African villages, generations of African families were torn apart, and life for African men, women, and children would never be the same.

I didn't know it at the time, but present-day marine archaeologist David Moore was studying the slave trade and had gotten wind of the English Wreck. Because so many shackles were found underwater in a single location, David suspected, like Moe, that New Ground Reef might be the site of a shipwreck that had been part of the 17th-century transatlantic slave trade.

Ten years had passed since Moe Molinar had discovered the shackles from the English Wreck. David was surprised that no one had yet examined the shackles. They felt it was an injustice to let those relics be forgotten and fade away like something swept beneath the carpet of time and history.

He took on a mission to learn everything he could

about the English Wreck. He was beginning an amazing journey, and little did I know that I would soon be part of it. David and I believed that to understand our past—the people, cultures, and rationale for slavery—is to also understand ourselves. And so, in some ways, to David archaeology is also about the future and learning from our mistakes.

But David needed more information—a name, a date, a timeline—anything solid that could help him trace the origin of this shipwreck.

For that, David would need to strap on his wet suit and do a little underwater detective work.

BY THE START OF THE 16TH CENTURY, ACCORDING TO SOME HISTORIANS, TENS OF THOUSANDS OF AFRICAN PEOPLE HAD BEEN TRANSPORTED TO EUROPE AND ISLANDS IN THE ATLANTIC OCEAN.

CHAPTER 4

─────⚬~⚬─────

Wisdom does not come overnight. ~ Somali proverb

LATE ONE AFTERNOON

in July 1983, David Moore was aboard the *Trident,* peeling off his sea-worn wet suit.

For days, David had worked with other divers to survey strategic sections underwater looking for one important yet elusive piece of evidence: the ship's bronze sailing bell. He assumed that like most ships there would be a bell that would bear the name of the vessel—a vital clue that would help them unravel the mystery of this shadowy shipwreck. They needed this piece to start to put together the puzzle and confirm their theories about the ship's origins.

David was tired and a bit anxious. But then, as he emerged from the water, he heard one of his crewmates yell: "Hey, you're not going to believe this. I think we found something big!"

David rushed to the front of the boat, grabbed his dive gear, and stepped into the Gulf of Mexico. The other divers quickly followed.

On the seafloor, one crewmate led the group to an unexplored section of New Ground Reef where, buried in the sand and crusted over, there was a large object. David smiled through his dive mask.

It took a team of three men to hoist the heavy bell onto the *Trident* and place it in the middle of the deck. After several minutes of staring at the bell in disbelief, everyone started laughing and clapping and high-fiving and reveling in the most significant find from the English Wreck.

The bell was 13 inches high, and two-thirds of it was covered in limestone, which had helped protect it from the salt water.

But David, having studied the history of similar ships, recognized this as a specific kind of bell, a watch bell, which sounds every half hour to signal crew changes aboard a ship. Watches on deck are changed every eight bells.

David reached for a screwdriver (hey, not all archaeology is about delicate brushes and picks) and began to chip away at the thick coating on the bell.

As he scraped the hard, green layers away, a number slowly appeared. A "9." During the next few minutes, another "9" appeared, and then a "6," until a full date was showing on the bell: "1699." Everyone crowded around as David turned the bell around and started scraping the other side.

Slowly, one by one, bold letters began to appear until the crew was able to read the words that were inscribed on the bell:

HENRIETTA MARIE

CHAPTER 5

A friend is someone you share the path with. ~ African proverb

THIS IS
WHERE I enter the story.

It was 1992 and I was in Key West, Florida, to attend a conference for the National Association of Black Scuba Divers, an organization founded the year before by Dr. José "Doc" Jones, a world-renowned marine biologist and celebrated underwater explorer.

I was a newspaper reporter, but I had grown up and finally learned to dive. I had become an avid scuba diver, in fact, and that spring I had received a newsletter from the National Association of Black Scuba Divers announcing plans to dive over a slave ship.

Doc was sitting alone in a corner of the conference hotel scribbling notes on a yellow legal pad and watching his dream of a black scuba-diving organization become a reality as black people from coast to coast began to check in at the hotel's front desk.

Why did Doc decide to establish a *black* scuba-diving organization, you might ask? Well, scuba diving can be a risky sport, and it's incredibly important for scuba divers to be able to rely on their dive buddies underwater. Their lives might just depend on it.

Over the years, some black scuba divers have been dismissed because of the color of their skin. It happened to me in Florida, about 20 years ago, when a white diver refused to dive with me because he assumed, since I was black, that I didn't have diving experience and that I would jeopardize his safety underwater. Honestly, that made me worry that he would jeopardize *my* safety underwater. After getting the newsletter from the National Association of Black Scuba Divers, I decided to join.

The weird part, I discovered later, was that apparently I wasn't actually on the list of newsletter recipients, and no one was sure how I had happened to receive the newsletter.

At the hotel in Key West, Doc invited me to pull up a chair and join him, and we talked for two hours. He told me about his vision for bringing black divers together, and he was passionate about sharing the news about the slave ship. He was excited that I was a journalist and hoped I might help tell the story of this ship.

"It's an interesting coincidence that this slave ship has come to our attention at a time when we're forming a national organization of black scuba divers," Doc said.

Doc talked about possibly being able to lay some sort of underwater memorial at the site of the *Henrietta Marie*.

I couldn't wait to be a part of this historic slave-ship pilgrimage.

I also wanted to learn everything about this ship— who the owners were, the manufacturers of the shackles and the cannons, the captain, the crew—and more about this gruesome business of slavery. I have to admit, a part of me wanted to direct my anger at someone, but I also wanted to understand. How could people do this to others? And how could they get away with it?

So I turned to Corey Malcom, another marine archaeologist with deep knowledge of the *Henrietta Marie,* for answers. Corey was introduced to the *Henrietta Marie* in 1986 when he saw the shackles from Moe's discovery in a laboratory in Florida. In 1991, Corey led an excavation to the *Henrietta Marie.*

I told Corey that I also wanted to know and visit the places where the *Henrietta Marie* anchored. By going there, I felt I could be closer to my own ancestry and past.

Retracing the route of a slave ship was more than a history lesson for me: This was an emotional journey. I had a deep yearning to know more about the oppressed African people aboard the *Henrietta Marie* because, as an African American, I feel they're part of my heritage.

I realized I would never know the names of the African people aboard the *Henrietta Marie,* but I couldn't help wondering: Was it possible that any of my ancestors had been on this slave ship? Even though that was a long shot, chances are they were brought over on a ship very similar to this one. Did they think they would see Africa again?

To learn more about the ship, the people on board, and my history, I knew I had to stop what I was working on and focus my attention on this. I knew I had to retrace the *Henrietta Marie's* steps.

In October 1994, I headed to London to begin my journey.

CHAPTER 6

If you close your eyes to facts, you will learn through accidents.
~ African proverb

DAVID, THE ARCHAEOLOGIST

who helped discover the *Henrietta Marie*'s watch bell, and I agreed to meet in London. I knew we'd make a great research team: He was a thorough scholarly researcher, and I could use my strengths as a journalist to dig up clues and interview experts and anyone else who could help us piece together the story of the slave trade from 300 years ago.

David was in London ahead of me. At the time, he was researching 17th-century slave ships and, in particular, the infamous pirate Edward Teach, better known as Blackbeard. David was working from the sprawling National Maritime Museum in Greenwich, England, a suburb of London, and was fast becoming one of America's foremost authorities on Blackbeard.

I met David at the National Maritime Museum on a sunny Monday morning. The museum was impressive: It was a magnificent structure of white pillars, sky-high ceilings, cherrywood shelves, and shiny hardwood floors, a place where scholars and historians read and studied the world through books, old newspapers, and documents—a perfect place for us to start.

When I finally found David, he was hunched over a long wooden table in a far corner of the museum. Unsurprising to me, he was surrounded by stacks of books (some even in other languages), cluttered papers, and a jumble of his own handwritten notes.

"Well it's about time," David said, as he looked up at me and grinned.

David and I are completely different: He's white, I'm black; we are both from the U.S., but David is from the small-town South and I'm from the urban North; David likes reading and research, and I like to talk to people and interview folks. Yet here we were, two men with totally different perspectives coming together in pursuit of one amazing mission: to discover this ship's story and, in so doing, shed some light on the history of the slave trade.

David started acquainting me with his mounds of paperwork. Among the documents, there were shipping records that showed the *Henrietta Marie* docked along the Thames River in East London in the late 1600s.

And there was centuries-old material that listed the names of the *Henrietta Marie's* three captains— William Deacon, Thomas Chamberlain, and John Taylor—on ancient records that detailed the *Henrietta Marie's* slaving voyages. When one captain died or fell ill, another captain would take over the helm of the *Henrietta Marie.*

I learned that the *Henrietta Marie* is the oldest sunken slave ship ever excavated in the United States and one of only a handful of slave ships found worldwide. David and Corey had explored the *Henrietta Marie* shipwreck together in 1993 and reached the same conclusion: This ship truly was an extraordinary find.

According to British historian Nigel Tattersfield, the *Henrietta Marie* is believed to be the world's largest source of tangible objects representing the early years of the African slave trade, including the largest collection of slave-ship shackles ever found on one site—enough shackles to restrain as many as 325 African people on a single ship.

Flipping through the notes David had gathered from British historians, I learned that the ship was probably built in France and had come into the possession of the British in the late 17th century, most likely one of almost 1,300 prizes captured from the French during King William's War. Despite the fact that Henrietta Marie was the name of the daughter of King Henry IV of France, who had reigned from 1625 to 1649, it is believed that the vessel was named for the wife, sister, or daughter of someone who owned the ship.

The earliest known date of operation for the *Henrietta Marie* as a slave ship was in 1697, and the ship made at least two slaving voyages carrying Africans to the West Indies. Through shipping records, we learned that on the first voyage, which lasted until 1699, the *Henrietta Marie* delivered more than 200 African people to Barbados to be sold as slaves.

As I read more about the *Henrietta Marie*, it was hard for me to stay detached, even though the long-ago writers of these records seemed to be objective, merely stating the numbers of slaves as if they were barrels of oats. I felt so angry but also so incredibly sad for these people—my people.

"The *Henrietta Marie* has always taken a backseat to the wreck of the *Atocha*—the treasure that was found in that wreck fired up people's imaginations, but the artifacts from the *Henrietta Marie* were just stuck in a corner in the museum," David said.

"As an archaeologist," he said, "I attempted to view the site as objectively and as scientifically as possible. But when you look at those shackles, what that ship was doing—her objective—really hits home. Those shackles haven't been handled by more than one or two people since they were worn by slaves."

Also recovered from the *Henrietta Marie* were thousands of glass beads. Some of them—the ones with large stripes—were called "gooseberries." The tiny glass beads were made in Venice, Italy, and they were a variety of colors: dark blue, bright yellow, turquoise, green, and white.

They were undoubtedly beautiful, though they were cheap to make and cheap to buy. They became a valuable commodity to slave traders for one important reason: The beads were precious to Africans and were used to barter for African people who would be traded into slavery.

Some African medicine men used the beads for healing, and artists fashioned the beads for sculptures. Some African kings strung the beads together and wore them to symbolize political and social power; some kings adorned their bodies with so many beads that aides had to help them stand from their thrones because they were so heavy.

The little beads quickly became a significant part of West African culture. As beautiful and important as they must have been, I wondered how they could have measured against a human life. Textiles and other manufactured goods, including weapons, were also used to buy African people. But these little beads became legendary because they were so insignificant outside of the slave trade. To people today, it makes no sense.

I spent my days inside the National Maritime Museum studying books about slavery. If I was going to figure out what happened with the ship, I'd have to do a lot of research. Before being in that library, I hadn't realized there were so many books about the African slave trade.

Through reading countless entries from these historical books, captain's logs, and journals, I slowly came to grips with the fact that slavery, for ship

SLAVERY WAS INDEED AN INTERNATIONAL BUSINESS ...

captains, was simply business, nothing more. Even though I understood this concept from an intellectual perspective, it was still difficult for me to read about more atrocities, in the name of business, every time I turned a page.

As I read the journals, I was struck by what I didn't see: the word "human" to describe African people. Instead, there were words like "beasts," "savages," "merchandise," "creatures," "pickaninnies," and "cargo."

Slavery was indeed an international business—but I believe it was a business based on racial injustice, because the main "cargo" shipped to the New World was boatloads of African people.

But sheer curiosity and a need to understand spurred me on. I kept reading these journals. Like this detailed passage from *Slave Ships and Slaving* by George Francis Dow:

From 12,000 to 15,000 slaves were exported annu-ally from this locality, during periods of years, the English, French and Dutch participating in the trade. These slaves were brought down the rivers from market towns, a hundred and more miles away, having origi-nally come from considerable distance in the interior.

Some were undoubtedly prisoners of war but many were kidnapped by raiding parties ... The arms of some of the men would be tied with grass rope ... they were ironed, or chained, two together ...

And then, through research, again offered by Nigel Tattersfield, I learned about Anthony Tournay.

Tournay was a successful ironmonger and shackle maker who provided the *Henrietta Marie* with 33 tons of iron, and historians believe that Tournay supplied the slave ship with some of the shackles before it sailed from London to Africa.

I started tracking Tournay's 300-year-old footsteps and became more distressed with each discovery. He was a prominent and influential businessman in London who was respected in the British community where he lived and worked. He lived in luxury on famed Thames Street and traveled around London in a sparkling horse-drawn carriage. At night, his dining room table was well lit by silver candlesticks. Tournay arranged for his servants to be paid for two years after his death, and he gave generously to charities.

During his life, he amassed considerable wealth, but it was from trading for African people. I never read anywhere that Tournay was apologetic for his dealings in human trafficking. African people aboard the *Henrietta Marie* suffered—and many surely died—while wearing the shackles that Anthony Tournay manufactured specifically for them.

I know things were different back then, and many things we know are abhorrent today were accepted, but still I just couldn't imagine crafting thousands, maybe hundreds of thousands, of shackles knowing they were for human wrists.

I was surprised to learn that Tournay, whom I decided was a cold-blooded businessman, had compassion for the underprivileged children who lived in London. Tournay died in 1726 at age 76, which was quite a ripe old age for the time. He left 100 pounds sterling (a considerable sum back then) to

St. Thomas Hospital to educate poor children.

As I read about Tournay's legacy, a myriad of questions raced through my mind: Why did Tournay care about the British children but was not concerned about African children who were handcuffed in his chains? Why did he treat his servants well but offered no sympathy for the African people he knew were suffering in slave ships? Why was he comfortable living in grand style knowing that African people aboard the *Henrietta Marie* were separated from their families forever and many would never live to see the New World?

There were so many questions about Tournay and so few answers. I was slowly coming to despise a man I had never met, and I was also becoming more emotionally drained.

I didn't know if I would ever get all the answers I was seeking, but my questions led me down a narrow street, around a corner, and to the front steps of a redbrick building in the heart of London.

I paused for a moment before opening the heavy wooden door. I was anxious about what I might find inside.

CHAPTER 7

There can be no peace without understanding. ~ Senegalese proverb

I STOOD ALONE ON THE STEPS

outside the open doors of the St. Mary Abchurch chapel, slits of sunlight filtering gently through the stained-glass windows.

I couldn't seem to get my feet to budge.

I wasn't sure I wanted to know what was inside this centuries-old house of worship that has been standing since 1681.

And I wasn't even sure I was in the right place. I had read conflicting information about where exactly Anthony Tournay was buried, but I wanted to visit the grave site of the man who manufactured those shackles for the *Henrietta Marie*. Shackles that were used to confine possibly hundreds or even thousands of African people on a journey into cruelty and bondage.

I had read that some of London's more prominent citizens were buried beneath St. Mary Abchurch in the 17th century, many of them undoubtedly having ties to the slave trade—and that maybe Tournay was one of them.

I finally took a deep breath and walked in. I walked through the silent church and found stairs that led to a dark hallway lined with long gray tombs along the floor and pressed into the walls. It was difficult to read the names on the crypts since they were faded by decades of dust and sediment.

"May I help you?" a cleric asked.

I told him that I was looking for a particular crypt, and with a sudden burst of emotion, I revealed that it wasn't a family member—that it was not a friend.

The cleric said that so many people had been buried beneath the church over the years that bodies were stacked on top of each other and it would be impossible to know exactly who was entombed here. Any records of burials, he explained, would have been lost decades ago.

"Good luck with your travels, my son," he said. "I hope you find what you are looking for." He then left standing me alone in a room filled with crypts.

I had come to St. Mary Abchurch out of some desperate need to understand, as though somehow being near Tournay would bring closure and end the circle of hate.

I found, despite my best intentions, I wasn't ready to forgive. I was mad. And I was frustrated. I stomped the stone floor, thinking maybe, just maybe, Tournay was lying beneath me.

I was angry for all the Africans aboard the *Henrietta Marie* who could not voice their own anger. I was angry for the millions of Africans taken from their homeland to a terrifying new world where they were treated with cruelty and hatred.

I was trying to look deep within myself to find forgiveness, but it wasn't easy. I walked out of St. Mary Abchurch and found myself just lingering outside on the steps once again. I hadn't found the closure I had been seeking, but I did have a renewed sense that in order to get some sort of closure I needed to know more.

I went back to the library, back to the papers, but the research experience was painful and beginning to take its toll. Not because of the density and number of books and papers that I was reading, but emotionally.

I couldn't seem to read about slaving in one sitting; I would constantly get up from the library table and take a walk outside to get some fresh air.

A friend I had made while I was in London handed me a book called *Equiano's Travels.* It was a remarkable manuscript written by a once enslaved African named Olaudah Equiano, who in 1789 published an account of his life—from being kidnapped in Nigeria, to slavery in the West Indies, to finally winning his freedom.

According to his book, Equiano was born in 1745 and was a member of the Igbo tribe. He was captured in Nigeria when he was 10 years old and wrote about the terrible conditions aboard a slave ship. Many historians say his book, *Equiano's Travels,* is the only story ever written that documents the voyage on a slave ship to the West Indies from the perspective of an African.

From Equiano's book and from other research, I knew that space aboard the *Henrietta Marie,* like that on other slave ships, was extremely tight. I knew slave ships were cramped, but I was surprised—and bewildered—to learn about the systematic packing techniques by slave traders to fit as many African people into the hull of slave ships as possible.

In his book *Sins of the Fathers: A Study of the Atlantic Slave Traders, 1441–1807,* James Pope-Hennessy wrote, "Sometimes the ships filled quickly, and the wooden shelves, which the carpenters erected in the holds now empty of European merchandise, would be crammed with Negroes lying, as we have seen, like books upon a shelf ..."

There was no room for Africans to stand in the lower decks of the *Henrietta Marie,* and sometimes they were forced to remain in chains, on their sides, for much of the entire voyage, which could last months. There was not much fresh air, and Africans were only sporadically allowed on deck for a glimpse of sunlight.

I could only imagine what it must have been like to have a normal life in your village and then suddenly be kidnapped—stolen away from your mom, dad, sisters, brothers, and grandparents—and then brutally forced down into a dark hull of a ship where you're shoulder to shoulder with hundreds of frightened strangers who might not even speak the same language or dialect as you, and you have to wear painful iron chains day and night. It smells awful, there's nowhere to go to the bathroom, and this goes on for months. And you have no idea where you're being taken. To see people being whipped, beaten, and even killed around you, and hearing the desperate sobs of women and children and men who, like you, will never see their families again.

Africans who attempted to escape—or revolt—were thrown overboard, a powerful reminder for others to remain submissive. Despite myths that enslaved Africans were passive and willingly allowed themselves to be kidnapped, there were actually hundreds of slave revolts on the high seas.

But historian Nigel Tattersfield, who did extensive research about the *Henrietta Marie*, believes there were no slave revolts aboard this particular ship.

Back in London, we had learned that William Deacon was the first captain of the *Henrietta Marie*. He was 30 years old when he took over the helm, which was young for a ship captain, but Deacon already had practical experience. He had captained at least two other slaving voyages aboard the *Crown* slave ship that delivered about 305 African men and women to Barbados on April 22, 1695, and 211 African people in 1696.

As the first captain, there certainly would have been a lot to do to get the *Henrietta Marie* ready to set sail. In the late 1600s, Deacon walked the docks along the Thames River beside the anchored ship, searching for a crew to sail with him for Africa. He would find a ragtag crew of questionable characters near Execution Dock, the place where the infamous pirate Captain Kidd was hanged in 1701.

Deacon would have needed a carpenter, a sailmaker, a ship's surgeon, a cook, a gunner and his mate, an accountant to keep the ships' records, and seamen. Records show he found 18 men in all who were prepared to sail to Africa. And, in addition to all this, he would have needed guns, fresh water, long knives, tobacco and rum, and shackles—lots of them—for wrists, necks, legs, and ankles.

Deacon also ordered eight large iron cannons installed on the ship to protect against pirates, who often commandeered slave ships during voyages.

We reviewed records that showed Deacon pulled away from the dock in Wapping, East London, and sailed along the Thames River and out to the English Channel, bound for West Africa, on November 10, 1697.

Deacon was at the helm of a 120-ton wooden ship designed with iron spikes (as a form of armor) that was built for speed under six canvas sails. The hull of the ship was configured to hold about 300 Africans to make a three-month journey from Africa to the West Indies. This was the *Henrietta Marie.*

I had learned all these important facts about the ship, but I still had so many questions. Where were the cannons manufactured? And who made them? Did that person know what they would be used for? How could someone be the owner of a business to manufacture such a thing? I needed to find out.

Chapter 8

To get lost is to learn the way. ~ African proverb

SEVERAL DAYS LATER, my research partner, David, and I were speeding through the English countryside in the rain with a burly Scotsman named Angus behind the wheel.

"Jeeps are made for hard driving!" said Angus, with a thick accent, as he raced into Sussex County. David was quiet, no doubt hoping we would arrive at our destination safely.

Angus Konstam is a noted historian and author of some 70 books who is known for his groundbreaking research on 17th-century weapons—and, as we learned, for his legendary heavy foot on the gas pedal.

From shipping records, David and I found out

there were eight cannons on board the *Henrietta Marie*. These cannons were six feet long and weighed between 750 and 1,000 pounds each. The cannons had all been marked with an "S."

Based on his research, Angus believed that the cannons were made at a foundry, or metal factory, called Stream Mill, which had manufactured 450 tons of iron guns during the 17th century. We found records that the mill had been located outside the hamlet of Chiddingly, but we didn't have anything else to go on. The only thing we had was a weathered book Angus had found in the library that had a 300-year-old black-and-white drawing of what Stream Mill looked like in the late 1600s. It was certainly a long shot.

Angus believed that the cannons were made for John "Mad Jack" Fuller, a local landowner who also owned a plantation in Jamaica. We speculated that enslaved Africans from the *Henrietta Marie* were taken there to work the fields.

As Angus swerved along rocky roads and rustic dirt paths, wind whipped through the canvas top and mud splashed against the sides of the car. Wet shrub branches occasionally clawed against the sides. I looked out at the sodden landscape before me, softly rolling green hills disappearing into the mist and fog. Even drenched, it was a breathtaking and mystical scene. It was getting later in the day, though, and we still hadn't found the mill.

And then, suddenly, while racing down a bumpy hill, Angus slammed on the brakes and we came to a complete stop in the middle of nowhere.

"I need to check the map," said Angus. I started to wonder if Angus was relying just on gut instinct up to this point.

He reached into the glove compartment and unfolded a large, crinkled paper map with highlighted yellow markings on wiggly red lines.

"Are we lost?" I asked.

"Have a lil' faith, will ya?" Angus said, with a grin.

I needed to find the mill. I wanted to stand where the factory once stood, walk where these factory workers once walked, and try to make sense of it all.

"We'll keep driving," Angus said. "It's out here somewhere."

AS ANGUS SWERVED ALONG ROCKY ROADS AND RUSTIC DIRT PATHS, WIND WHIPPED THROUGH THE CANVAS TOP AND MUD SPLASHED AGAINST THE SIDES OF THE CAR.

A little while later, Angus came out of yet another gas station with another map. He explained that sometimes these local county maps were a bit more thorough, and could include historical locations and neighborhood landmarks that larger maps would miss. We spread it out on the front of the car and each scanned a portion of the map.

"Here it is!" Angus exclaimed.

In the middle of the map, in tiny letters that could be easily overlooked, were the two words we had longed to see: *Stream Mill.*

It was positioned on the map near Chiddingly, just like the records had said. We hopped back in the car and Angus started the engine, gunned the gas, and took off down a dirt road.

After a little while, Angus veered off the main road and onto a series of smaller lanes that seemed to get narrower with each sharp turn until we steered onto a one-car gravel lane. This led to a two-story stone house with a heavy wooden front door that looked a lot like the old-world houses in the books from the library.

Angus pulled into the stone-covered driveway and turned off the engine. We all stared at the book from the library and compared the 17th-century drawing to the live landscape in the distance.

"This is it! We're here!" Angus said.

"So what do we do now?" David asked.

"We knock on the door!" Angus responded. "We're likable guys."

We had no idea how the homeowners would respond to a colorful group of men at their doorstep at dusk and full of inquiry. "Hi, we're looking into the history of a 17th-century slave ship and that brought us to your property!" Right.

Angus knocked and we all stood on the steps waiting for somebody to answer. In just a few seconds, a thin, middle-aged woman opened the door. She had little smile wrinkles at the corners of the eyes.

"May I help you?" she asked.

Her name was Marilyn Ambroziak, and she lived on the spacious property with her husband, George. They had converted the house into a comfortable bed-and-breakfast that was noticeably off the beaten path.

"We hope we're in the right place," Angus said. "We're looking for the old Stream Mill foundry."

"Well, you're in the right place," Marilyn said. "This was a foundry in the 1600s. I don't know how you found it."

CHAPTER 9

The friends of our friends are our friends. ~ Congolese proverb

AS I LOOKED AROUND,

there were no houses for miles around. I could hear dogs barking in the distance.

We told Marilyn about our quest to learn the complete history, down to the cannons, of this shipwreck.

"Come with me," she said. "I'll show you around."

I was amazed. Growing up in Detroit, if three strange men had come to my door near dark claiming to be doing research, I'm not sure what my mother would have done, but she almost certainly would not have invited them in!

But this was rural England, and fortunately Marilyn was intrigued with our investigation.

Marilyn escorted us to the side of the house where a 10-by-10-foot sealed area was layered with bricks.

"This is where the foundry and the furnace used to be," she said. "Our house was built over it."

We learned that the foundry had four-ton crescent-shaped hammers that were powered by water paddles and pounded hot iron at 150 strokes a minute.

As I walked along the property, I could feel the crunching of glass bottles under my feet. Marilyn explained that these were 17th-century ale bottles, tossed to the ground by Swedish laborers who were brought in to work in the foundry casting iron cannons.

Marilyn laughed. "We used to think it was fascinating from a historical perspective to find old ale bottles from the 17th century all over the yard, but now they're just a pain!" she said.

Then she took us through a maze of soggy soil and rain-soaked shrubbery nearly 50 yards from the house. As we peeled the looming branches away, we saw a little stream with a light current. It was the stream for which the mill was named, and it all suddenly looked a lot more like that drawing we had.

As we stood there by the stream, which winds all the way to London, Angus explained that the mill workers would send the big, heavy guns downstream, which was easier than transporting them over land.

Angus explained that during the casting process, workers at this mill would mark the cannons with an "S," like signing their name on their work. This was a huge breakthrough for us. It seemed we had found our foundry.

It was dark as Marilyn led us back to her house.

For weeks, I had waited to find some kind of tangible connection to the *Henrietta Marie*, not just mere speculation. But now, I felt we were getting somewhere and all of our research and detective work were finally paying off.

I still had so many questions, though. From our research, we knew that John "Mad Jack" Fuller had owned the land the foundry was sitting on back when it was operational. We knew he had owned several plantations in Jamaica and eventually moved there to oversee them—and the Africans working them.

But who was he?

CHAPTER 10

Learning expands great souls. ~ Namibian proverb

I WAITED FOR A FLOCK

of black-bellied sheep to cross the road in Bridgetown, Barbados, before I could walk into the Department of Archives and continue the next stage of my research.

Back in London, I had learned that the *Henrietta Marie* anchored in Carlisle Bay, a harbor in Barbados, on July 9, 1698.

By the time the *Henrietta Marie* arrived in the West Indies after its first slaving voyage to Africa, she was a storm-battered ship creaking in the harbor. The three-month voyage from West Africa had taken its toll on the ship, its crew, and the enslaved Africans, many of whom died during the Atlantic crossing.

The Department of Archives in Barbados is located near the banks of the Atlantic Ocean. It is a breath-taking site, with azure waters that stretch outward from pristine white sand beaches. It looked like a tropical paradise, but I couldn't help thinking about how it became a living hell for untold numbers of enslaved Africans.

I brought along photocopies from slaving journals to compare to research material I found in Barbados. Shipping records from the late 1600s indicated that the *Henrietta Marie* delivered "250 negro slaves and 150 elephants' teeth" here as part of its first voyage.

Glorious humans and magnificent animals perished. Did the people involved in the slave trade really think this was okay?

I reviewed Nigel Tattersfield's research: Barbados was the *Henrietta Marie*'s first port of call, and the African men and women were sold at public auction. Of the some 250 slaves on board, more than half of them—188—were consigned to a wealthy slave merchant named William Schuller.

Schuller was a prominent Barbados citizen who paid an average of £19 for each enslaved African—

a total of £3,589. After being invasively inspected, the "healthy" Africans were taken to a nearby warehouse where they were forced to work the sugar plantations in Barbados—cutting down sugarcane stalks from dawn to dusk.

I was captivated by the islands in the Caribbean and how they played such a major role in the history of the *Henrietta Marie.*

Sugar, nicknamed "white gold," was a lucrative business in the Caribbean back then, and the African labor force was an important backbone of the Caribbean's commerce and profit margin.

Because of this, slave owners were incentivized to get the most labor possible out of each worker. They were not tolerant or understanding. They forced African men and women to work sometimes 16 hours a day in the sweltering sun.

And there were a lot of rules. Africans were not allowed to practice their rituals from Africa; they were not permitted to attend religious services in Barbados; and oftentimes they were not even allowed to speak to one another.

Reviewing further notes from Tattersfield, I found

an account by a missionary named Father Labat who visited Barbados around the time the *Henrietta Marie* anchored in Carlisle Bay in 1698.

He wrote:

The English take very little care of their slaves and feed them very badly ... The overseers make them work beyond measure and beat them mercilessly ... and they seem to care less for the life of a Negro than a horse.

I read documents that said Schuller belonged to the Gentleman of Vestry, a town council in St. Michael's Parish. Schuller would often loan out his African "property" to St. Michael's Parish to work on road repairs.

A document from the 1700s listed two enslaved Africans, "John the Negro," who was baptized in the mid-1700s at the age of 40, and "William the Negro," who was buried in the mid-1700s. Both men, according to the documents, were the "property" of Schuller. The timing fit into my puzzle. These men could have sailed on the *Henrietta Marie*.

I thought about men like Schuller and wondered about their motives. He belonged to a parish, which presumably preached good deeds, but he practiced cruelty toward humans. Was he motivated only by greed? Did he ever show any remorse for his inhumane treatment of these African people?

My second day in Barbados, I woke up to the sun piercing through my hotel window. I was anxious to get away from the library for a day and explore Carlisle Bay.

I wasn't sure if I'd find any artifacts in the bay after all these years, but it was important for me to retrace the route of the *Henrietta Marie,* to dive in the same waters where the slave ship sailed and to walk the land where enslaved Africans from the *Henrietta Marie* were sold to Barbados businessmen.

It was probably largely symbolic, but it was something I had to do.

As I walked along the ocean's shore, I saw black children walking to school and younger kids playing in the sand, and I thought about the generations of African families that were torn apart by slavery.

"Hey, mon, are you ready for some good diving?" my dive guide asked with enthusiasm.

My guide took me to a spectacular coral reef.

Besides sea turtles, seahorses, and even a shiny barracuda, I saw broken ale bottles, chunks of broken anchors, and rusty pieces of iron. Who knows if any of those relics were from lost slave ships, but I did know that I was swimming in the same waters where the *Henrietta Marie* docked with 250 African men and women all those years ago.

Diving here did not clear my head. It only had me asking why again and again. And so, early the following morning over coffee and toast, I studied my notes, unfolded my map of the Caribbean, and decided to plot my course again. I had to continue to retrace the slave ship's route. Next port of call: Jamaica.

CHAPTER 11

Peace is costly but it is worth the expense. ~ Kenyan proverb

THE HENRIETTA MARIE ARRIVED

in Port Royal, Jamaica, on May 17, 1700. This was the second slaving voyage for the *Henrietta Marie*.

As I reviewed the shipping records, I saw that the ship had moved on to its second captain, John Taylor, after Deacon had given up his command several months earlier.

This time, after an arduous three-month voyage from Africa to the Caribbean, there were only 190 Africans on board—90 men, 60 women, 30 boys, and 10 girls—shackled in the cramped, foul-smelling hold beneath the ship. Two days later, they were led off the *Henrietta Marie* in chains, down a gangway, and into the town square of Port Royal.

Some of them were branded with the letters "H-M" to identify them as having come from the *Henrietta Marie* slave ship.

Like in Barbados, these Africans were rounded up by European slave owners who bid on them like cattle. The men were sold for £18 each, the women £16, the boys £14, and the girls £12.

I couldn't stop thinking about those tiny shackles made for tiny wrists. I thought about my daughter, Ariane, and her tiny wrists. It broke my heart to imagine girls like her chained aboard a slave ship and then sold at public auction into a brutal life of slavery.

At the end of the year in 1700, the *Henrietta Marie* plotted a course back to England and sailed away from Jamaica. The route would take the ship past the Cayman Islands, around Cuba's Cape St. Antonio, and across the Florida Straits, a dangerous stretch of water that slave-ship captains liked to avoid.

THE MEN WERE SOLD FOR £18 EACH, THE WOMEN £16, THE BOYS £14, AND THE GIRLS £12.

From David's research and Nigel Tattersfield's notes, I finally discovered what had happened to the *Henrietta Marie.* While sailing the Florida Straits, the *Henrietta Marie* likely collided with a ferocious hurricane that tore the wooden ship apart. The crew dropped all of the ship's anchors in a desperate attempt to ride out the storm, but the hurricane was too powerful, even for the 120-ton ship.

The crew were all washed over the side of the ship and were never seen again. And all of the chains, shackles, and manacles used to restrain African people fell hard to the ocean floor, where they rested for 300 years until they were discovered by Moe Molinar, the black treasure hunter.

I found it to be some sort of cosmic justice that just the crew had encountered that fearsome hurricane. But I couldn't help wondering if maybe it would have been better if the Africans had perished as well—to save them from the cruel fate that awaited them.

I had to keep digging. I had to know what had become of the enslaved Africans and where they had gone next. I knew from research that Fuller, the cannon maker, owned a plantation located in a rural area of Jamaica, not far from Spanish Town. That would be my next destination.

‿‿‿

CHAPTER 12

It is not what you are called, but what you answer to.

~ African proverb

SPANISH TOWN WAS A DUSTY, congested place

with constant bumper-to-bumper traffic. The town square was a mess of broken bottles and overgrown weeds. A once beautiful white-domed building in the middle of town had become a crumbling structure with peeling paint and shattered windows, a common refuge for drifters.

David and I began our research on Fuller's plantation in a long-standing archival building in Spanish Town, in the parish of St. Catherine, near Kingston, where "Mad Jack" Fuller owned his plantation in the late 1600s and early 1700s.

Spanish Town is the former capital of Jamaica and is far off the beaten path for tourists today. The town was established by the Spanish in 1534 but was taken over by the British in 1655. Like most of the Caribbean, it has a long history of colonization—and it shows.

There are large areas of poverty, and the city has a reputation for high crime. Guides were highly recommended, but David and I were two confident guys and decided to venture into Spanish Town alone.

The archival building is a place where official records are stored. David and I had pulled onto a busy street near the library where a dozen or more young black Jamaican men were hanging out.

There was a rusty, wrought-iron gate that separated us from the library, and as we walked through it, the young Jamaican men out front became curious about our visit; they stared at us from the curb and asked for money.

David and I continued inside where we were greeted by a woman asking how she could help.

We explained that we were looking for any information about the Fuller family from the 1600s and 1700s, and the Knollis Estate, which from our research we knew to be a 1,500-acre parcel of land that had once been part of Fuller's plantation and had been transformed into a rugged sugar plantation that still existed.

The woman was gone for about 20 minutes and returned with two dusty leather-bound books and the words "Probate Records" barely visible on the front. The date on the books was 1745.

David's inner archaeologist came out as he whispered to me that these books—records of wills from people who had died centuries earlier—had not been properly preserved over the years because the pages were worn. Despite that, surprisingly, the handwritten entries were still legible.

Between the brittle pages we read that the Fullers were prominent people on the island of Jamaica in the 1700s. They were influential landowners, lawyers, and judges who were desperately trying to hold on to their land—and their African slaves.

In a handwritten letter from Stephen Fuller, one of John Fuller's sons, we saw that he'd written to Jamaican authorities asking for protection.

He said enslaved Africans had begun to outnumber white residents on the island, "a vast disproportion between Negroes and whites," and the Fuller family seemed worried about being harmed by the very people whom they had brought over by the boatload all the way from Africa to work their plantations.

I was immensely curious about this present-day property that was once owned by the Fullers, so the next day David and I hired a driver to help us find the Knollis Estate. The driver was Jamaican, had grown up near Spanish Town, and knew the area well.

The Knollis Estate was still listed on Jamaican maps, so we plotted our course and headed into the shadow of Jamaica's Blue Mountains.

We drove for about 45 minutes, past horse-drawn carts, past young men selling jerk chicken on the side of the road, and past little Jamaican boys and girls in blue-and-white school uniforms.

Turning down a bumpy road, we saw a sign for the Knollis Estate, and I got out of the car and knocked on the door of a modest house behind a small church, hoping the person inside might be able to offer more information.

An elderly gentleman with thin gray hair and a friendly smile answered the door. I told him I was looking for the Knollis Estate. He pointed down the road and told me that part of the old Knollis Estate

I WAS IMMENSELY CURIOUS ABOUT THIS PRESENT-DAY PROPERTY THAT WAS ONCE OWNED BY THE FULLERS ...

had been renamed the Tulloch Estate. The community surrounding the estate was called Bog Walk.

I had photocopied pages with me from a history book with drawings that showed what the Knollis Estate had looked like in the 1700s. But I had no idea what it would look like today.

I learned that the present-day Tulloch Estate had been transformed into a banana-packing farm. Once I reached the estate, I looked around at acres of Jamaican men and women picking and packing bananas. A man driving a tractor said to me, after I asked about life there, "It's been hard sometimes. But we make do." Then he told me something really extraordinary: "There's an old Jamaican family that's been around for years," he said. "They live down the road. Their name is Fuller."

CHAPTER 13

A family tie is like a tree, it can bend but it cannot break.

~ African proverb

BLACK FULLERS?

I was curious to learn about the Jamaican Fullers. In the 1700s, during slavery, it was customary for slave owners to give their last names to their African workers. These could very well be living, breathing descendants of the *Henrietta Marie* slaves.

So for the first time on my journey, after all my research, travels, and studying of history books, probate records, wills, and death certificates, I felt that I was on the brink of a phenomenal discovery.

As a seasoned journalist, it was important for me to conduct my research in London and Jamaica, but it was something extremely powerful to potentially meet and interview people who could be real-life links to this long-lost ship.

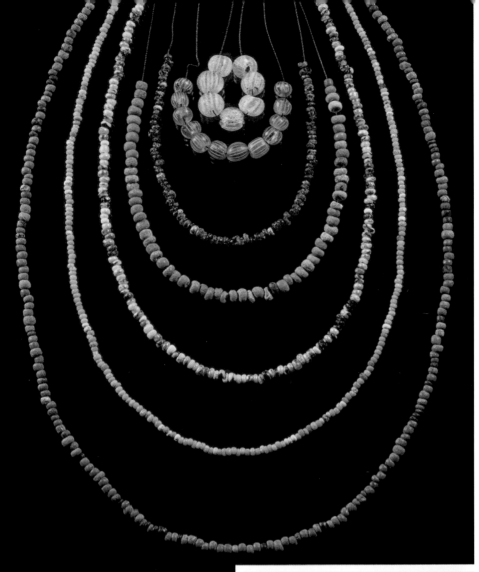

ABOVE *These easily manufactured and seemingly insignificant glass beads took on an important role during the years of the slave trade: They were used to barter for African lives.*

RIGHT *Historian and underwater archaeologist David Moore holds an elephant tusk, encrusted in sediment, recovered from the* Henrietta Marie *wreck site.*

ABOVE *Fort of Gorée Island, today a UNESCO World Heritage Site, located off the coast of Senegal. This is an outpost that also includes the infamous "House of Slaves," which is where some Africans were kept before they were boarded on ships headed to the New World.*

BELOW *Historian and underwater archaeologist David Moore (right) examines the hull of the* Henrietta Marie.

LEFT Historian and underwater archaeologist Corey Malcom studies the hull of the Henrietta Marie.

BELOW The bronze bell of the Henrietta Marie

BELOW Michael Cottman gently touches the underwater memorial, which honors the African lives lost during the passages of the Henrietta Marie.

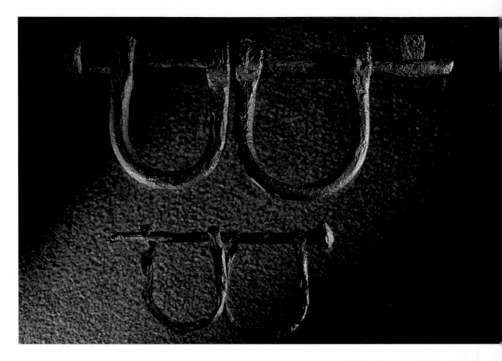

ABOVE *Just some of the dozens of iron shackles recovered from the Henrietta Marie wreck site. These iron bars were efficient, unyielding, and sure to cause those who wore them discomfort and even pain.*

ABOVE *Spoons recovered from the Henrietta Marie. An encrusted spoon lies above a cleaned one.*

ABOVE *An encrusted cauldron that historians believe was used to cook yams or beans for the slaves aboard the Henrietta Marie*

I knew it was unusual, but I had this strange sense that, whether or not these people were actually distantly related to me, they were my family. I would never know for sure if my ancestors were aboard the *Henrietta Marie*—but I did know one thing: In the face of so much despair, cruelty, and sadness, these people and I were all connected because we had survived. Our people had survived.

I pulled out my notebook and walked to the front porch of a small, peeling, clapboard house where a black man with a mop of white hair and green eyes introduced himself as Colin Fuller and welcomed me into his home.

And then he told me his story.

"I was born right out back," said Mr. Fuller, pointing to the lush backyard of his modest home.

Mr. Fuller said when he was 18 years old, in the 1920s, he used a machete to cut sugarcane for his British bosses who owned the Tulloch Estate. He said he worked 12 to 14 hours a day and was paid about 10 cents a day for his work.

Over the years, he said, he buried four brothers and four sisters in Bog Walk, not far from the Tulloch

Estate, and even though he didn't move around very well anymore, he recalled the days of harvesting tobacco and sugarcane.

Colin Fuller explained that his nephew, Larkland Fuller, could fill in more gaps. Since he lived across the street, I headed there to learn more. Larkland told me that for 30 years he hauled bananas from the fields on the Tulloch Estate, but he felt he wasn't treated fairly and was underpaid; even after 30 years of working on that estate, he was only paid 50 cents a day.

Historians believe the Knollis Estate may have originally been as large as 5,000 acres and Mad Jack Fuller likely could have taken Colin Fuller's ancestors from the *Henrietta Marie* to the Knollis Estate in the 1700s. The timing made sense.

As I walked off the property, I stared at the old peeling warehouse that was once used as a barracks for the enslaved Africans who worked the plantation. I felt trapped in a time warp.

After talking with the Jamaican Fullers, I felt like I finally had some closure, but there was still one thing I had to do.

CHAPTER 14

A patient person never misses a thing. ~ Swahili proverb

I COULDN'T LEAVE JAMAICA
without going
for a dive. I wanted to feel the water around me, a
cleansing force, and float, weightless, in the same
waters where the *Henrietta Marie* had docked back in
1700—the legendary docks of Port Royal.

The next day, I loaded my gear onto a dive boat. I
was headed into an infamous part of the *Henrietta
Marie's* past.

When we arrived at the dive site, I peered down
the side of the diving boat and into the water. I saw
the shadowy outline of a 300-year-old city. In 1692,
an earthquake triggered a tsunami that submerged
part of Port Royal underwater. This underwater

portion is called the Sunken City. I had read about it in old library books, but I was eager to experience the eerie underwater town for myself. This was the site where the *Henrietta Marie* anchored—and where the enslaved Africans were led down the gangway into this terrifying new world.

"Welcome to the Sunken City, mon!" the boat captain said in a thick Jamaican accent.

I zipped up my wet suit, strapped on my scuba tanks, and rolled backward off the dive boat. The water was warm, and I could see a few nurse sharks on the seafloor. They watched our trail of bubbles.

As I descended slowly into the harbor, I could see the rubble and cobblestone streets that were still preserved from the earthquake. It was like swimming in a giant museum of crumbling brick and debris, over the remains of Lime Street where pirates once swaggered through the streets; pirates like Blackbeard, whom David had studied, and Calico Jack, who became famous for designing the Jolly Roger flag—the dreaded skull and crossbones that identified pirate ships.

Around me underwater, and wedged into the sand, was handcrafted pottery that had survived the earthquake. I swam along the broken streets, past cracked brick walls and a splintered staircase, part of a town that had crashed into the sea and been frozen in time.

As I swam among the bright-blue parrotfish and a school of delicate yellow angelfish, I thought about the *Henrietta Marie* and the African men, women, and children being hustled off the ship. I imagined their fears and confusion.

What were their thoughts aboard this slave ship? Did they have hopes that they might see their families again? What did they think was waiting for them when they docked?

As I thought about these questions, I realized my journey to retrace the route of the *Henrietta Marie* wasn't over yet. I couldn't end here. After all, this was only a stopping point along the journey of the ship and so it would be for me. I needed to travel to Africa, where it all began.

CHAPTER 15

Traveling is learning. ~ Kenyan proverb

IN THE DAYS

that followed after Jamaica, I prepared for a trip to Africa, where the *Henrietta Marie* sailed the coast, its crew trading for African people. Africa was critical for my research, but it was also important for me personally. As an African American, Africa is part of my lineage.

I started brushing up on my French and finally boarded a nine-hour flight to Dakar, Senegal.

The day I landed, I took a walk along the shoreline in Dakar, where I was greeted with an array of aromas.

I smelled saltwater air blowing in off the Atlantic Ocean; I breathed in the sweet-smelling incense that old men burned in makeshift kiosks on the side of the road; I smelled rice and roasted meat that women in colorful robes cooked on hot grills under canvas tents; and I smelled fresh-cut flowers that children sold to foreigners at bustling intersections.

"Bonjour," a tall, dark gentleman said to me.

This poised, tall (about six-foot-seven-inch) man was going to be my guide and translator for my 10-day visit to West Africa.

"I'm Ibrahima Top," he said with a wide smile. "Everyone just calls me Top, but if you prefer Ibrahima, that is fine, too."

"Please call me Michael," I said.

I liked the name Ibrahima; it had a regal ring to it, much like Ibrahima himself. He was quiet, laid-back, and extremely knowledgeable about Africa, its history, its culture, and its people. I soon learned he was a devout Muslim and had earned a master's degree in history. He spoke several languages fluently, including French, English, German, Italian, and Wolof, a native West African language.

"I understand you want to visit Gorée Island?" Ibrahima asked me. "I can take you. But come quickly, the ferry gets very crowded."

Gorée Island was known to be a brutal, inhumane

slave port, one of the first places in Africa to be settled by Europeans and the Portuguese in 1444.

Gorée is also known as the House of Slaves, or the "Door of No Return." Today it serves as a museum and memorial for the untold numbers of enslaved Africans who were held in crammed stone cells and herded through this location before being hauled onto slave ships that were anchored offshore.

Historians say the Door of No Return was given its ominous name because it was the last time that African people would see their homeland again as they were dragged into a life of slavery.

Scholars believe the *Henrietta Marie* may have anchored off the coast of Senegal before heading to Calabar, in present-day Nigeria.

Here I was standing on the shores of my ancestral homeland, and I was filled with a range of emotions. I felt extreme sadness for my African ancestors who were forced into the brutal slave trade, and anger at the European slave traders, but uplifted by the enduring spirit and survival of African people.

I hoped by being here, as an African American, that it would be like my ancestors were finally

I HAVE ALWAYS BELIEVED MY SPIRIT— AND THE SPIRITS OF ALL AFRICAN AMERICANS— IS AN EVERLASTING PART OF THE CONTINTENT.

coming home. I wanted to reconnect the severed ties of my African lineage. I wanted to visit the Senegalese waterways where the *Henrietta Marie* had sailed, to give names and personal histories to face-less Africans and, ultimately, to pay homage to the suffering and courage of my ancestors.

In some small way, I have always believed my spirit—and the spirits of all African Americans—is an everlasting part of the continent. Our ancestors endured the worst possible fates imaginable— and we survived.

Chapter 16

A wise person will always find a way. ~ Tanzanian proverb

AS WE WAITED to board the ferry

to Gorée, I watched young African boys swimming in the sea, a rhythm of black arms in synchronized strokes. Beautiful dark-skinned women in colorful robes and embroidered jewelry carried straw baskets on their heads; old men with gray hair sat near the beach playing West African board games; and young men asked for dollars in exchange for watching them dive from the side of the ferry into the sea.

"I am glad you are in Africa to learn how to tell our story," said Ibrahima, as a gathering of African children followed us around the island. "I have watched many African-American people come here to cry."

I waved at a group of children who asked me if I was American.

I tried to fool them.

"Bonjour!" I said. And they laughed and ran away.

Ibrahima helped me get acquainted with a new land. "Speaking French will get you whatever you need, but speaking Wolof will earn you the respect of Senegalese people," Ibrahima said.

"French is not our language. Wolof is our language, and Wolof should be your language while you are in Senegal. Wolof is the language of your people, and you should speak your family's language."

I told Ibrahima I would like to learn some Wolof during my stay in Senegal.

"When do we start my lessons?" I asked.

"Immediately!" Ibrahima responded.

"When we say 'Hello, how are you?' we say *Nang-ga-def.*"

I repeated very slowly, "Nang-ga-def."

"Good," Ibrahima said.

"Now when we say 'I'm fine, thanks,' we say *Mangi-fi-rek.*"

I repeated, "Mangi-fi-rek."

"Very good," Ibrahima said. "Now, when we say 'thank you,' we say *Jerry-jef.*"

"And if you want someone to leave you alone," Ibrahima explained, "you say firmly, *May-ma-jam!*"

I didn't think I'd need that. I was here to welcome Africans back into my life, not to have them leave me alone. It turned out Ibrahima knew more about what I needed than I did myself.

When we arrived at Gorée Island, we walked for about 30 minutes along the dusty streets and arrived at the front of a two-story building where a large sign was written in French: *Maison des Esclaves*—House of Slaves.

A short, gentle, dark-skinned man wearing a cap and sunglasses opened the large door. He was an older man but he had plenty of energy—and loads of knowledge. He looked a lot younger than his 74 years.

"Hello, I am Joseph Ndiaye," the man said. "Welcome to Gorée Island."

He had a firm handshake—the kind of handshake my father always told me reveals a man's character.

Mr. Ndiaye was the curator of Gorée's House of Slaves. But he was much more than just a curator—he was a Senegalese intellectual institution.

Everyone in Senegal knew about Mr. Ndiaye; he

was celebrated by dignitaries, loved by children, respected by historians, and admired by educators. He would often gather children to share the history of Gorée Island, visit schools, and lead young people on tours of the Door of No Return.

I followed Mr. Ndiaye on a tour of the House of Slaves.

Mr. Ndiaye explained that the House of Slaves was built in 1526 and was the only original slave house left on Gorée Island. The largest room was for men; it held about 25 men for up to three months. Slave owners would lead the African men into the cramped room, chain them, and leave them sitting in the sweltering cells until the slave ships came.

"They were treated like animals," Mr. Ndiaye said.

"Europeans took the best of what Africa had to offer," he said, "stripped us of our strongest people, depleted our resources, disrupted our civilization, and separated us from our families."

People sometimes wonder why Africa today is considered such an underdeveloped continent. It's not so surprising when you consider centuries of European plundering, kidnapping, and ransacking of villages.

As I looked around, Mr. Ndiaye asked if I needed some time alone. Suddenly I realized that's what I wanted—*needed*. I had to reflect and take it all in. I thought it was a very empathetic question and nodded. *May-ma-jam*, I needed to be left alone.

As he walked away, I thought about the enslaved Africans who were alone, who were now nomads on the high seas; I thought about the *Henrietta Marie* alone at the bottom of the ocean; and I thought about the loneliness felt by African mothers and fathers, husbands and wives, sons and daughters. But it's the collective survival of African people that has shaped this profound part of our history.

Alone, I walked around the grounds, very slowly, as if there were people around me. I peered into the dark, cramped stone cells; I didn't want to step inside, but I did anyway. What would I feel inside the dark prisons? Anger? Sadness? Would I be unforgiving?

It was difficult to breathe because there were no windows, no breezes of fresh air, and no sunlight. I thought about how horrible it was for the men, women, and children who suffered in these stone rooms.

I was surprised to find myself suddenly kneeling on the floor, brought to my knees in grief.

The House of Slaves was quiet with only a few tourists left by the end of the day. I walked through the courtyard and through the archway of the Door of No Return. I stared out into the Atlantic Ocean where slave ships were anchored offshore 300 years ago.

As my thoughts were focused on my African ancestors, I could hear Mr. Ndiaye talking to a group of tourists behind me.

He explained later what he had told them: "Today, there is a young man, a writer, an African American, standing behind you who has returned home to Africa. He has returned home to write the story of his ancestors because his roots are in Africa and he is connecting with his African family," Mr. Ndiaye said. "And because this African-American writer has returned home to us, I can no longer call this doorway the Door of No Return."

Chapter 17

If you want to go quickly, go alone.
If you want to go far, go together.
~ African proverb

IT WAS GETTING DARK

and Ibrahima, who was extremely patient, reminded me that the last ferry leaving Gorée Island would be leaving soon, so we should begin our walk back to the dock.

"I'd like to share something with you before you leave," Mr. Ndiaye said.

Mr. Ndiaye pointed to an array of historical photos in his office. "I grew up in this house," he said, as he pointed to one building on the yellowed photograph.

"This was a slave house like many others," he said. "I lived here from the age of nine until I was 14. My mother and father lived upstairs and I lived downstairs. Downstairs was very dark. Today, this house is a symbol of the atrocities that black people endured."

I shook Mr. Ndiaye's hand.

"Jerry-jef!" I said, proudly speaking Wolof.

Mr. Ndiaye laughed and grabbed my arm.

"You're welcome!" he said in English. And he joked about never retiring as the curator of the House of Slaves.

"You have a big day tomorrow," Ibrahima said. "You will be scuba diving on Gorée Island, right?"

I nodded.

Of course, like the other places where the *Henrietta Marie* had been, it wasn't enough to walk the land. Like the ship, I had to get in the water.

CHAPTER 18

Return to old watering holes for more than water;
friends and dreams are there to meet you.

~ Swahili proverb

THE NEXT DAY.

I arrived at a small, rustic dive shop in Dakar surrounded by huge baobab trees that lined the streets of the city.

"Bonjour!" a stocky man with muscular arms and a deep tan yelled from the top of the steps. It was the owner, Haidar. He wore a faded baseball cap and baggy shorts, and he had rugged hands, the hands of an old-school scuba diver.

I explained to Haidar that I wanted to dive at an area outside Gorée Island, a site where numerous slave ships anchored over the centuries and where untold numbers of African people lost their lives, both literally and figuratively.

Gorée Island was not on Haidar's list of dive sites for his customers, and frankly he was a bit baffled that I wanted to dive a site that was not known for the area's best scuba diving. Eventually, Haidar led me to the dock where his small, wooden, single-outboard engine boat was tied to the pier. We loaded the dive boat with our gear and after a few minutes on the ocean we could see Gorée Island in the distance.

"We will be there in 15 minutes," Haidar said. "I will say when to get ready."

As we got closer to Gorée Island, I could see the Door of No Return from a different perspective: This time, I was looking at the Door of No Return from the viewpoint of the African people who were seeing their homeland for the last moments as they sailed away from Africa on slave ships.

Haidar tossed the rusted anchor over the side of the boat. We were anchored just offshore facing the House of Slaves and I could look through the Door of No Return.

"Is this close enough? Haidar asked.

"Yes," I responded.

"Then whenever you're ready," Haidar said.

I rinsed my mask, strapped on my scuba tanks, buckled six pounds of lead around my waist, slipped on my fins, set my dive watch on "dive mode"—and prepared for a dive that was more about my ancestral past than marine biology.

I splashed into the Atlantic Ocean. The water was warm and murky. As I slowly descended to 30 feet, I could barely see Haidar through the maze of silt but he motioned me to follow him closer to Gorée Island.

As I drifted in the current, I closed my eyes, just for a moment, to reflect on this once-in-a-lifetime experience: swimming underwater possibly in the same seas where some of my African ancestors were engulfed by rising tides, and where they glimpsed their homeland for the last time.

When I opened my eyes, I saw spotted stingrays buried in the sand around me; I saw a baby octopus with its tentacles reaching out from a cracked glass bottle; I saw the rusted broken butt of an old rifle that was wedged in the sand; and I wondered if it was a weapon from a slave ship.

As I exhaled underwater, I finally released some of the anger toward the European slave traders who

... I FINALLY RELEASED SOME OF THE ANGER TOWARD THE EUROPEAN SLAVE TRADERS WHO HAD KIDNAPPED AFRICAN PEOPLE.

had kidnapped African people. I was beginning to find some peace as I thought about the beauty of the African continent and the resiliency of my people.

As the currents gently washed over me, I glanced at my dive watch—I had been underwater for 64 minutes, although my extraordinary experience scuba diving in Africa felt like it had happened in the blink of an eye.

And before surfacing from beneath Gorée Island, I reflected on the words that Mr. Ndiaye had said to me outside the House of Slaves: "You have returned."

CHAPTER 19

A friend is someone you share the path with.

~ Tanzanian proverb

I WAS BACK

in the U.S. after my trip to West Africa and was still sleeping when the telephone rang.

"So how was your trip to Dakar?" a man asked.

The inquisitive man on the other end of the phone was Dr. José "Doc" Jones, that world-renowned marine biologist, celebrated professor of marine science, world traveler, co-founder of the National Association of Black Scuba Divers—and my mentor and friend.

One year had passed since Doc offered his ambitious idea to place a one-of-a-kind underwater monument on the sunken wreckage of the *Henrietta Marie* slave ship.

In that time, Doc had assembled 12 scuba divers, archaeologists, and scholars to help make his idea a reality. Included among that group were, of course, Corey Malcom and David Moore.

Our plan was to place the monument on the ocean floor, but it wasn't so simple. Because of swift currents and potential hurricanes, the monument would need to be constructed out of concrete to ensure its longevity. I was overjoyed at the thought of participating in this underwater remembrance of the African slave trade—to not allow history to forget these African people once again.

That May I walked into the Mel Fisher Maritime Heritage Society in Key West, Florida—where the artifacts from the *Henrietta Marie* are stored—and asked the receptionist for the two marine archaeologists, my friends Corey and David.

Corey, by that time director of archaeology, met me in the lobby of the museum. He had grown a beard since the last time I saw him, but he still looked like a young man even in his early 40s.

"How are you, Mike?" Corey said, with a friendly handshake. "I know you'll be interested in all the work we've been doing on the *Henrietta Marie*."

I followed Corey to his office, which was situated

in the sprawling conservation laboratory.

The lab is a place where underwater archaeological artifacts, many from shipwrecks, are stored and preserved; these included some of the rusted shackles from the *Henrietta Marie.*

Shipwrecks are often referred to as "moments in time" or underwater "time capsules" that often contain information about the people onboard the vessels during sailing years.

Corey explained that the Mel Fisher Maritime Heritage Society had a large collection of historical relics in the laboratory, including gold and silver bars and coins; precious jewels; various metals; glassware and ceramics; ivory, wood, seeds, insect fragments, bones, and leather. The objects range from cannons, crossbows, and other weaponry to tools, ship's rigging, hardware, navigational instruments, personal items, galley utensils, shackles, trade goods, and coin chests.

Corey said that each material requires specific treatment for preservation, and treatments may vary between a few hours to several years depending on the type of material.

Corey explained that this process, which preserves

cultural property found in the sea from further deterioration, is called conservation.

Corey's desk looked like a shipwreck itself—there were crumbled maps with squiggly lines identifying long-ago shipwrecks strewn over his desk; steel scuba tanks leaned against the walls; wet suits were hanging in the corner; and all sorts of small artifacts filled his bookshelves, which were jam-packed with almost every book about archaeology imaginable.

Corey pointed to a long, gray tank where a pair of shackles from the *Henrietta Marie* were being well maintained.

Corey casually said something then that had a profound meaning for me. He said, "These shackles are an important part of our collective history."

I looked at him and mulled his words over. His phrasing, "our collective history," was pivotal for me to hear because we came from different racial and ethnic backgrounds, but it was true—this was about *our* past.

And for the first time that anyone could recall, African-American scuba divers and white marine archaeologists were coming together to examine a sunken slave ship and pay tribute to enslaved

Africans—black and white underwater explorers united by the same passion and purpose. We were learning about and making history.

At dinner that night, we divers all spoke about the various reasons we were there to help place the memorial. We all brought our stories and we all had our reasons. My buddy Hank Jennings, Jr., talked about why he planned to dive to the *Henrietta Marie* site.

Hank lost his mother to cancer in 1985. His father, Hank Jennings, Sr., a police officer with the Hartford Police Department in Connecticut, died at 28 years old in 1964. He was the first police officer killed in the line of duty in the department's 103-year history.

Hank's father was an accomplished swimmer and an enthusiastic scuba diver, and he taught Hartford teenagers to scuba dive. One newspaper described Hank Jennings, Sr., as a person who tried to bring all members of the community together "despite the racial tensions of the day."

Hank Jr. was only seven years old when his father died, and his dad never had the chance to teach Hank to swim or scuba dive.

In some ways, scuba diving on the *Henrietta Marie*

gave Hank an opportunity to share a special moment underwater with the memory of his father.

"I'm here because of him," Hank said. We were there not because of the history I'd traced, but because of all our own unique histories, so many stories that came together to make one history.

After dinner, we all walked back to the hotel and Doc pulled me aside.

"I'd like you to chronicle this dive for us," Doc said. "You're the writer. I know this is a special dive, and I don't want this dive—and what it means to African-American people—to end up underwater in the sand for another 300 years."

I was honored by Doc's request.

"This is a rare opportunity for us, you know," Doc said softly. "We don't know if some of the slaves on the *Henrietta Marie* were members of our family. They could have been. But we do know that this is the first time that black divers have ever researched their history—in this way—underwater. We're literally diving into our past."

CHAPTER 20

For tomorrow belongs to the people who prepare for it today.

~ African proverb

MORNING CAME QUICKLY.

It was time to dive.

At 5:30 a.m. the sun made its first appearance as we loaded our dive gear onto our boat, the *Island Diver,* donated for our use that day by Dr. Robin Lockwood, a local physician and owner of a Key West dive shop.

Ten of us headed out to New Ground Reef. We were a quiet group that morning.

I found a corner of the boat and started scribbling notes into my journal. The journal that contained notes from so many journeys and so many stories— but none touched my heart and soul as much as this story.

It was getting full and I had only a few pages left, so I started scribbling notes in the margins and on the backs of used-up pages.

As the *Island Diver* bounced across the waves, I looked up and stared at a beautiful clear blue sky.

"Ten minutes to the site!" the boat captain shouted. "Get ready!"

I was.

CHAPTER 21

The eyes that have seen the ocean
cannot be satisfied by a mere lagoon.
~ African proverb

"**WE INVITE** God's presence to join us as we pay homage to our forefathers whose fateful voyage on the *Henrietta Marie* through no choice of their own brought us back to this place," Bill Murrain, my friend and a fellow diver and lawyer from Atlanta, said to our group. "We stand on the shoulders of those who preceded us to honor their memory and to make this world a better place."

As I descended into the Gulf of Mexico, the warm currents on New Ground Reef pulled me 300 years into another era.

I wasn't thinking about fish or sea turtles or sharks on this dive; I was thinking about the enslaved African people who were held captive aboard the *Henrietta Marie*.

Doc and David carefully lowered the one-ton concrete memorial onto the ocean floor. They positioned
it facing east—toward Africa.

I watched as David and Doc, a white man and a black
man, gently placed the monument on the ocean floor.

I swam around the memorial, touching it gently. I
studied the bronze inscription on the monument.

"HENRIETTA MARIE: IN MEMORY AND
RECOGNITION OF THE COURAGE, PAIN, AND
SUFFERING OF ENSLAVED AFRICAN PEOPLE.
SPEAK HER NAME AND GENTLY TOUCH THE
SOULS OF OUR ANCESTORS."

In my head, I recited an African prayer I had stumbled
upon in my research and wondered if any of the
African people aboard the *Henrietta Marie* whispered
the same prayer before they went to sleep.

Bless us.

Bless our land and people.

Bless our forests with mahogany, wawa, and cacao.

Bless our fields with cassava and peanuts.

Bless the waters that flow through our land.

CHAPTER 22

He who learns, teaches. ~ Ethiopian proverb

AND WHAT DID I LEARN?

What did we learn collectively from the *Henrietta Marie* slave ship?

Dr. Madeleine Burnside, a former executive director of the Mel Fisher Maritime Heritage Society, said that she wanted to use the *Henrietta Marie* story to expose the mind-set of the Europeans who benefited from the African slave trade.

"There were people who made choices—the men who arranged for the pewter (metal mugs and plates), and the wives who packed the pewter in the crates. Did the wives know that these crates were going on a slave ship?" Madeleine asked.

"Where did the wives think the money to buy new

dresses came from?" she asked. "The *Henrietta Marie* has reminded us of how much we don't know about this part of history, how much we need to learn, and how much research there is to do."

Indeed, there is much more research to do. And my journey exploring stories behind the *Henrietta Marie* doesn't end here.

In 2001, David and Corey revisited the *Henrietta Marie* wreck site—but this time to bear witness as they uncovered a portion of the actual ship. I was there, too.

The hull had been found and Corey and David wanted to scientifically examine the wreck and, for the first time, photograph and film the uncovering of the *Henrietta Marie.*

Using powerful dredging equipment, Corey and David held large exhaust hoses that sucked sand from the ocean floor and slowly exposed the hull. It took about five hours.

It was tedious work, but it was well worth the wait.

Thirty feet beneath the sea, I hovered over the *Henrietta Marie* wreck and knocked on the hull with my knuckles. The hull was as hard as a rock after being preserved by sand and limestone for 300 years.

And in the blink of an eye, all of this weighty history rushed through my mind: from shipping records in London, to the shores of Gorée Island, to meeting the black Fullers in Jamaica.

I wasn't turning the pages of books anymore, I was actually touching the *Henrietta Marie,* a vital part of global history, and, for African Americans, a relic of a painful past.

Underwater, with my chest pressed against the ocean floor, I ran my hands through the grains of sand and plucked tiny blue, yellow, and purple beads from the ocean floor. Yes, they were the beads that Europeans used to trade for African men, women, and children along the coast of West Africa. These tiny, beautiful, insignificant beads that came to have so much importance.

I had learned so much from my years-long odyssey over three continents retracing the route of the *Henrietta Marie* slave ship.

I had learned that the site of the wreck is a place where I am never really alone, a place where I feel connected to my past and ancestors. I had learned

"DO YOU BELIEVE IN FATE?" I ASKED HANK AS WE SAILED AWAY FROM NEW GROUND REEF.

that lasting friendships can be forged—regardless of racial backgrounds—even while exploring a sunken slave ship.

More than that, I had learned that I wanted to share this rich history with my daughter, Ariane, and her children, and on, so they can all embrace their history, too.

And although I had several leather-bound journals filled with research notes and thoughts, there were still questions that had gone unanswered.

"Do you believe in fate?" I asked Hank as we sailed away from New Ground Reef. "Did Moe find the *Henrietta Marie* slave ship? Or did the *Henrietta Marie* find us?"

Voyage to Discovery

KWADJO TILLMAN was just 11 years old when he pulled his mask over his thick clump of braids and plunged into the Gulf of Mexico to explore the wreck of a 17th-century slave ship.

Kwadjo, to date, is the youngest scuba diver ever to descend on the wreck of the *Henrietta Marie* slave ship. He was part of a group of 10 young inner-city African-American students from Nashville, Tennessee, who visited the sunken wreck site in 2005.

I watched Kwadjo, with his wide-eyed expression, become enthralled with the *Henrietta Marie* while he spent 20 minutes underwater reading—and admiring—the inscription on the monument. From that moment, I knew Kwadjo was destined to become an avid scuba diver.

"There is no better way to get up close and personal

with the sea than scuba diving," Kwadjo said.

Kwadjo's dive on the *Henrietta Marie* wreck was sponsored by members of the National Association of Black Scuba Divers (NABS), which later evolved into a partnership with the National Oceanic Atmospheric Administration (NOAA). The unprecedented joint venture became known as "Voyage to Discovery," an initiative to discover the untold stories and maritime achievements of people of color through education, archaeology, science, and underwater exploration. NOAA's Office of National Marine Sanctuaries works to get young people interested in ocean education. Scuba diving is an important economic activity for many coastal communities, and encouraging new scuba divers helps promote continued interest and participation in the sport.

"THERE IS NO BETTER WAY TO GET UP CLOSE AND PERSONAL WITH THE SEA THAN SCUBA DIVING."

Kwadjo was one of three young members of the National Association of Black Scuba Divers who traveled to the Thunder Bay National Marine Sanctuary in 2010 to participate in a scientific expedition of the *Montana* shipwreck, a 235-foot steamship lying fragmented and algae-covered on the bottom of Lake Huron for nearly 100 years.

Kwadjo worked side by side with underwater archaeologists as they searched for clues about the history of the ship, which caught fire and sank in 70 feet of water in an area known as "Shipwreck Alley" in 1914. Today, Kwadjo is 23 years old and works with United Way in Des Moines, Iowa, where he is developing a plan to end poverty in Iowa. But he still works in scuba diving when he can. "I live in Iowa!" he said, laughing about his landlocked state.

The Voyage to Discovery–NABS/NOAA partnership has evolved into a signature program, the annual "Youth Education Summit" (YES), where about 25 young people between ages 10 and 16 come together every summer to learn about scuba diving, marine conservation, marine biology, oceanography, and maritime heritage, and particularly about the contributions by people of color to the maritime industry.

And they also learn about the *Henrietta Marie*.

In his article "In Search of the Slave Ship *Henrietta Marie*," Corey Malcom, director of archaeology for the Mel Fisher Maritime Heritage Society, said the quest for more evidence is not over.

"Work on the site continues today," Malcom wrote. "In the case of the *Henrietta Marie*, it is known that six cast-iron cannons are missing, along with iron trade bars and many other ferrous [iron] components. Over 30 years after its initial discovery, the *Henrietta Marie* continues to be a vital and important part of our maritime past.

"It has made the mechanics of the transatlantic slave trade a tangible reality," he added, "and with new discoveries on the horizon, will further reveal the secrets of the past in its eloquently unique way."

I hope the next generation of young adventure-seekers—boys and girls—consider scuba diving, marine biology, and oceanography as they think about careers that can help preserve a fragile yet fascinating underwater ecosystem, and that will teach them more about our collective past.

Since three-fourths of the Earth is covered by water, shouldn't we make it a priority to explore our planet, our history, and particularly what's beneath the sea?

Further Reading & Other Resources

Interested and want to read more? Grab a parent and check out these books and websites!

BOOKS

Equiano's Travels, also known as *The Interesting Narrative of the Life of Olaudah Equiano, or Gustavus Vassa, the African* by Olaudah Equiano. Republished by Heinemann, 1969.

The only known document that chronicles the slave trade from the perspective of an African aboard a slave ship

James Cameron's Titanic by Ed W. Marsh. HarperPerennial, 1997.

A classic tale for young readers and adults

Manfish: A Story of Jacques Cousteau by Jennifer Berne. Chronicle Books, 2008.

A story about the world's most famous underwater explorer

The Slave Ship: A Human History by Marcus Rediker. Penguin Books, 2008.

A wonderful resource based on 30 years of research

WEBSITES

Amistad Case, *history.com/ topics/amistad-case*

The amazing story of the Amistad slave ship

The Last Days of Blackbeard, *smithsonianmag.com/ history/last-days-blackbeard -180949440/?no-ist*

The ultimate pirate tale

The Mel Fisher Maritime Museum, *melfisher.org*

A great resource for the Henrietta Marie slave ship, the Atocha treasure ship, and other shipwrecks in Florida

National Marine Sanctuaries, *sanctuaries.noaa.gov*

A great website to explain all things related to the ocean

Nautilus Live, *nautiluslive .org/people/robert-ballard*

A fascinating website that introduces readers to Dr. Bob Ballard, a pioneer of deep-water exploration

NOAA Education Resources, *education.noaa.gov*

A go-to educational site for NOAA's information on the ocean, marine life, weather, and climate

NOAA National Marine Sanctuaries: Shipwrecks, *sanctuaries.noaa.gov/ shipwrecks*

A great resource for shipwrecks

North Carolina Maritime Museums, *ncmaritimemuseums.com*

A premier website that details all the outstanding coastal exhibits at the North Carolina Maritime Museums

Real Pirates, *events .nationalgeographic.com/ events/exhibits/real-pirates*

An excellent introduction to pirates and the history of pirates on the high seas

SNUBA, *snuba.com*

An introduction to SNUBA, a fast-growing resort activity that offers underwater exploration without tanks in a fun, safe environment for the entire family

The Underwater City of Port Royal, Jamaica, *whc.unesco .org/en/tentativelists/5430*

A compelling story of adventure and the remains of an underwater city

INDEX

Acknowledgments

Keith and Yolanda, thank you for graciously opening your home for me to write this book while sitting along the banks of the Chesapeake Bay, taking in the spectacular waterfront view, and breathing fresh air blowing off the surf. Your serene setting provided the inspiration to tell the story of the *Henrietta Marie* and the slave trade for young readers everywhere. You offered me something rare: serenity. You are true friends. Blessings, Michael.

A special thanks to David Moore and Corey Malcom—the scuba-diving marine archaeologists who brought the *Henrietta Marie* to life; Angus Konstam, who taught me all about 17th-century weapons; Dr. Madeleine Burnside for her steadfast support; Dr. José Jones, Bill Murrain, and Hank Jennings, my longtime friends, fellow underwater explorers, and mentors on the *Henrietta Marie* journey; and the late Moe Molinar, who discovered the slave-ship shackles in 1972 so we could tell the story of the *Henrietta Marie* today.

127

PHOTO CREDITS

COVER: FRONT COVER (background), Bob Hemphill/Getty Images; FRONT COVER (CTR), Jonathan Blair/National Geographic Creative; BACK COVER (background), Simone De Negri/EyeEm/Getty Images; BACK COVER (CTR), Courtney Platt/National Geographic Creative; BACK FLAP (UP), Courtesy of Ariane Cottman; INTERIOR: 1, Jonathan Blair/National Geographic Creative; 2-3, Simone De Negri/EyeEm/Getty Images; PHOTO INSERT: page 1 (UP), Courtney Platt/National Geographic Creative; page 1 (LO), Courtney Platt/National Geographic Creative; page 2 (UP), officek_ki/ Getty Images; page 2 (LO), Courtney Platt/National Geographic Creative; page 3 (UP LE), Courtney Platt/National Geographic Creative; page 3 (UP RT), Ira Block/National Geographic Creative; page 3 (LO), Courtney Platt/National Geographic Creative; page 4 (UP), Ira Block/National Geographic Creative; page 4 (LO LE), Ira Block/National Geographic Creative; page 4 (LO RT), Courtney Platt/National Geographic Creative